TUNBRIDGE WELLS
IN OLD PHOTOGRAPHS

MRS RAGGETT in the office of Dipper, serving water from the chalybeate spring on the Pantiles, photographed by D.J. Johnson on 31 August 1932. On the wall behind the spring is the bronze relief commemorating the discovery of the waters by Lord North in 1606, designed by local artist Charles Tattershall Dodd Jnr (1861–1951).

TUNBRIDGE WELLS
IN OLD PHOTOGRAPHS

COMPILED BY

M.L.J. ROWLANDS AND I.C. BEAVIS

ALAN SUTTON

Alan Sutton Publishing Limited
Phoenix Mill · Far Thrupp · Stroud · Gloucestershire

First published 1991

British Library Cataloguing in Publication Data

Tunbridge Wells in old photographs.
1. Kent. Tunbridge Wells, history
I. Rowlands, Michael
942.2'38

ISBN 0-86299-663-5

Typeset in 9/10 Korinna.
Typesetting and origination by
Alan Sutton Publishing Limited.
Printed in Great Britain by
The Bath Press, Avon.

CONTENTS

INTRODUCTION

Every town has unique features that form a character distinct from all others, no matter how similar two towns might appear to the visitor. In Tunbridge Wells one of these features is also the reason for the town's existence. Although now the town could survive and prosper without the famous chalybeate spring, without it there may never have been a settlement here so close to the pre-existing towns and villages of Tonbridge, Frant, Eridge and Speldhurst. Although a few loosely scattered houses were here before the third Baron North rode by and discovered the chalybeate spring in 1606 while on a visit to Lord Abergavenny, reference to the famous well has ever since formed some part of the place's name.

The position of the ancient town of Tonbridge, just five miles away, is the reason for early references to the Wells at Tonbridge. Early literary works employed no unique name for the rapidly growing development. Doctor Rowzee's 1656 treatise on the waters refers to the place as Queene Maries Wells. Elsewhere there are references to it as Frant Wells; Frant being a village two miles to the south and near to Abergavenny's seat at Eridge. Celia Fiennes visited in 1697, referring in her account simply to 'Tunbridge the waters I have dranke many years with great advantage'. Increasingly in the eighteenth century the town's name began to stabilize, although inconsistencies of the period in spelling generally have left recorded references to Tonbridge, Tunbrydge, and Tunbridge, some of which refer to this town while others concern the elder town to the north. It was not until as late as the 1840s that the spellings of ancient Tonbridge and the new town Tunbridge Wells finally became standardized, at least partly due to adoption of the current spellings by the South-Eastern Railway Company. In April 1909 Edward VII assented to a change of name for the town in recognition of continued royal patronage since the time of Queen Henrietta Maria. The King preferred the style Royal Tunbridge Wells to the alternative of Royal Kentish Spa. Following the Local Government Act of 1972 the name was renewed in 1976 letters patent of Elizabeth II stating that 'We of Our especial grace and favour and mere motion do by these Presents ordain declare and direct that henceforth the area of the former Borough of Royal Tunbridge Wells shall be called and styled ROYAL TUNBRIDGE WELLS ...' The District now named the Borough of Tunbridge Wells is, of course, not to be confused with its regally-prefixed principal town.

Just as there might never have been a settlement here were it not for that continuing source of iron-impregnated — said to be health-giving — water, neither would the Wells have become the fashionable spa enjoyed by royalty, nobility, the infirm, gamblers, revellers and tourists. As more than two centuries separate the rise of the Wells from the growth of photography, no photographs here can show at first hand the heyday of the Wells, the rule of Richard 'Beau' Nash, and the illustrious visitors and residents. However, the importance of the chalybeate spring, the Pantiles and the Common can be reflected in a collection of photographs from the past century. Shown here too are the Tunbridge Wells developments away from the spring – the institutions, the shops, civic life, the town people and their pastimes.

To the local historian such old photographs are often of far greater value than drawings, paintings and prints. This is because, except for the unusual art photographs of men like Tunbridge Wells's Henry Peach Robinson, historical photographs are generally records unblemished by an artist's interpretation. Visual records before the photographic era commonly started as a sketch. The artist might later work up a painting based upon the drawing. Or an engraver might employ his burin to transform the original sketch into a printed form composed not of continuous tone but of lines and dots. It is not often that one can compare eighteenth- and nineteenth-century topographical engravings with the original drawings or paintings upon which they were based. However, careful comparison of engravings, original artworks and other contemporary evidence often reveals marked discrepancies. On the other hand, street scene photographs and photographs of events from the Victorian period usually preserve the scenes exactly as they existed, often in the tremendous detail possible with the large glass negatives and huge cameras then in use. A dated photograph is thus a valuable record showing precisely what existed or what happened at a particular date. Even undated views can be useful after a little research. For example, towards the end of this collection a photograph of the business premises of Stephen Carwood at 8 London Road is included. The view comes from an undated album published in about 1912. The only way to date the photograph was to examine it minutely for any useful evidence. Luckily, at the right of the view is a poster advertising a forthcoming public meeting. The combination of a magnifying glass, a perpetual calendar and microfilm of old *Kent and Sussex Courier* newspapers eventually revealed that the event was to be held on Wednesday 6 June 1900. Thus one can say that the photograph was taken probably in April or May of that year. This then gives us a record for May 1900 of whose business occupied 8 London Road, the goods they sold, the design of the shop front, the type of paving, the type of wall cladding that the building had, and all sorts of other data, significant and insignificant.

This selection of photographs drawn from the collections of Tunbridge Wells Museum and Art Gallery ranges in date from the pioneering work of Thomas Sims in the 1860s up until comparatively modern town views of the early 1970s. Five photographs in the book were taken in 1990 specifically for comparison to Victorian views of the same scenes.

Reference to a number of history books while researching captions often reveals disagreements between authors over the details of dates and events. Thus, while researching for this collection of photographs, we have endeavoured to use the earliest and most original evidence available, employing contemporary sources wherever possible.

BIBLIOGRAPHY

Some of these works are out of print. However, they should be available through libraries.

Anon. Various dates. *Kelly's Directory of Tunbridge Wells*. London: Kelly's Directories Ltd.
Anon. Various dates. *Royal Tunbridge Wells* (official borough guide).
Anon. 1892. *Pictorial History of Tunbridge Wells and District*. Hove: Walser and Grist.
Anon. 1982. *History of the Tunbridge Wells Cricket Club*. Tunbridge Wells: Tunbridge Wells Cricket Club.
Austen, B. 1989. *Tunbridge Ware*. London: Foulsham.
Barton, M. 1937. *Tunbridge Wells*. London: Faber and Faber.
Brackett, A.W. [1928]. *Tunbridge Wells Through the Centuries*. Tunbridge Wells: A.W. Brackett.
Britton, J. 1832. *Descriptive Sketches of Tunbridge Wells & the Calverley Estate*. London: Longman and Co.
Burr, T.B. 1766. *The History of Tunbridge Wells*. London: T.B. Burr.
Clifford, J. Various dates. *Clifford's Descriptive Guide of Tunbridge Wells*. Tunbridge Wells: J. Clifford.
Davis, T. 1976. *Tunbridge Wells – The Gentle Aspect*. Chichester: Phillimore.
Elers, F.W. [1910]. *A Record of 82 Years' Work at the General Hospital Tunbridge Wells*. Tunbridge Wells: A.J. Pelton.
Elwig, H. 1941. *A Biographical Dictionary of Notable People at Tunbridge Wells*. Tunbridge Wells: H. Elwig.
Farthing, R. 1990. *Royal Tunbridge Wells – A Pictorial History*. Chichester: Phillimore.
Fiennes, C. See Morris (1949).
Gaspey, W. Various dates. *Brackett's Descriptive Illustrated Hand Guide to Tunbridge Wells*. Tunbridge Wells: W. Brackett.
Gill, M.A.V. 1983. *Royal Tunbridge Wells in Old Picture Postcards*. Zaltbommel, Netherlands: European Library.
Gill, M.A.V. 1985. *Tunbridge Ware*. Aylesbury: Shire Publications.
Harker, M.F. 1988. *Henry Peach Robinson – Master of Photographic Art, 1830–1901*. Oxford: Blackwell.
Hepworth, M. 1974. *The Story of the Pantiles*. Royal Tunbridge Wells: The Pantiles Association.
Hetherington, K. 1987. 'John Brown: Victorian Dairyman and Baker of Tunbridge Wells', *Bygone Kent 8*, pp.723–6.
Hetherington, K. and Griffiths, A. 1986. *Old Pubs of Tunbridge Wells & District*. Gillingham: Meresborough Books.
Homan, R. 1984. *The Victorian Churches of Kent*. Chichester: Phillimore.
Kent and Sussex Courier newspaper.
Knipe, H.R. 1916. *Tunbridge Wells and Neighbourhood*. Tunbridge Wells: Pelton.
Martin, W.S. and Row, B.P. c. 1897. *Tunbridge Wells of To-day*. London: Beechings Ltd.
Mauldon, J. 1977. *Tunbridge Wells As It Was*. Nelson, Lancashire: Hendon Publishing.
Morris, C. (ed.). 1949. *The Journeys of Celia Fiennes*. London: The Cresset Press.
Newman, J. 1980. *West Kent and the Weald*. Harmondsworth: Penguin Books.
Payne and Son. 1990. Catalogue of the Bicentenary Exhibition of Payne and Son. Tunbridge Wells: Payne and Son (Silversmiths) Ltd.
Pearce, L. 1904. *Historical Associations of the Free Churches of Tunbridge Wells, &c*. Tunbridge Wells: Pearce and Co.
Pelton, R. Various dates. *Pelton's Illustrated Guide to Tunbridge Wells and the Neighbouring Towns and Villages, with a Description of the local Botany & Geology*. Tunbridge Wells: R. Pelton.
Pelton, R. Various dates. *Pelton's Shilling Directory of Tunbridge Wells*. Tunbridge Wells: R. Pelton.
Phippen, J. Various dates. *Colbran's New Guide for Tunbridge Wells*. Tunbridge Wells: J. Colbran.
Rowzee, L. 1656. *The Queens Welles. That Is, A Treatise of the nature and vertues of Tunbridge Water*. London.
Savidge, A. 1975. *Royal Tunbridge Wells*. Tunbridge Wells: Midas Books.
Sprange, J. Various dates. *The Tunbridge Wells Guide*. Tunbridge Wells: J. Sprange.
Strange, C.H. 1939. *The Jubilee of Tunbridge Wells as an Incorporated Borough*. Tunbridge Wells: Tunbridge Wells Borough Council.
Tunbridge Wells Advertiser newspaper.
Tunbridge Wells and County Magazine.
Waring, H.A. 1937. *The Story of the Church of King Charles-the-Martyr*. Tunbridge Wells: H.A. Waring.

SECTION ONE

Civic Life

THE TOWN CLERK, W.C. CRIPPS, reads the Charter of Incorporation of the Borough of Tunbridge Wells from the Town Hall in Calverley Road on 27 February 1889. The Charter had been brought by special train to the West Station, its arrival being greeted by a twenty-one gun salute on the Common opposite. A Grand Procession then escorted the Charter Deputation to the Town Hall through streets decorated with flags and triumphal arches.

ALDERMAN JOHN STONE-WIGG (1827–97), first mayor of the Borough of Tunbridge Wells, served from March 1889 to November 1891. As chairman from 1878 of the town's former local government he had opposed the campaign for incorporation, but he was responsible for a reversal of policy when he discovered that new national legislation would place non-incorporated towns at a disadvantage. Stone-Wigg presented the mayor's badge of office, seen here, and the mayoral chair that still dignifies the present Council Chamber.

THE TOWN HALL had been the home of the town's former government, a Local Board of twenty-four members elected only by owners and occupiers of land above a certain rateable value. Here, Alderman Stone-Wigg presides over a meeting of the Borough Council in the new Council Chamber of the Town Hall in 1891. The mace was presented to the Council by Aldermen Hori Pink and Philip Jackson at the Council meeting on 7 October 1891.

HENRY CHAMBERS, macebearer and Town Hall keeper for the Borough from the early days of incorporation until 1927. He is a familiar figure in civic photographs of this period. The gilt mace itself incorporates in enamel the royal arms, the 1889 and 1976 armorial bearings of the Borough, and the shields of Kent and Sussex. The stem has an entwined decoration of hop vines, fruits and symbols referring to the chalybeate spring. In honour of John Stone-Wigg's long service to the town, the enamelled monogram JSW is on the base.

JOSEPH CHAMBERLAIN'S PHOTOGRAPH of the inaugural banquet of Sir David Lionel Salomons (mayor 1894–5), held in the Great Hall for about 300 guests including the Lord Mayor and Sheriffs of London. During his term of office Sir David, a wealthy inventor living at Broomhill, Southborough, inaugurated the town's first electricity supply and organized the first 'Horseless Carriage Exhibition' in Britain at the Agricultural Showground off Eridge Road.

THE TOWN HALL, CALVERLEY ROAD, decorated for Queen Victoria's Diamond Jubilee on 22 June 1897. The day's events included a Grand Procession to the Lower Cricket Ground, on which was held a Great Public Demonstration with singing led by massed bands and a choir of 4,000 children. This was followed by Old English Sports, dancing, a concert and a firework display, all held on the Common.

THE MAYOR, ALDERMAN C.R. FLETCHER LUTWIDGE, lays the foundation stone of the Municipal Baths in Monson Road on the morning of Jubilee Day, 22 June 1897. The Baths remained in use into the 1970s when they were superseded by new facilities at the Sports Centre in St John's Road, completed in 1974. The Baths building was demolished in 1988 to make way for the new Monson House, an annexe to the Civic Centre.

THE DEPUTY MAYOR, ALDERMAN H.M. CALEY, reads the proclamation of the accession of King George V at the Pantiles on 9 May 1910. Below the balcony can be seen the body of firemen who, together with the Borough Police, led the procession of councillors between the three points at which the ceremony was performed, the earlier two being the Town Hall and the Lower Cricket Ground.

A PROCESSION MAKES ITS WAY along Mount Pleasant to the civic memorial service for the late King Edward VII held at Holy Trinity Church on 20 May 1910. The *Courier* newspaper declared that 'few persons will recollect any event in recent years which so profoundly stirred the inhabitants of Tunbridge Wells.' At the time of the procession all shops were closed and it was estimated that there were some 20,000 people out on the streets.

A PROCESSIONAL FLOAT created by the Royal Victoria Lodge of the Ancient Order of Druids stands outside the Grosvenor Hotel (at the western end of Calverley Road) ready for the Hospital Sunday church parade on 18 July 1909. The Druids were one of several friendly societies which organized these parades as an annual event to raise funds for local hospitals.

WILFRED CAFFYN OF KING CHARLES' SCHOOL dressed for his part in the civic procession celebrating the coronation of George V. The local schools had been asked to prepare a series of tableaux depicting events in British history, and naturally King Charles' had been allocated 'The Restoration of the Monarchy – The Entry of King Charles II into London'.

PART OF THE GEORGE V CORONATION PROCESSION passing along Mount Pleasant on 22 June 1911. In the foreground is the Tunbridge Wells Tradesmen's Association float, representing distinguished visitors to the Wells and featuring Beau Nash and Queen Anne. It is followed by the Fire Brigades of Royal Tunbridge Wells and Tonbridge and the Borough Police.

THE MAYOR, SIR ROBERT VAUGHAN GOWER, reads the Proclamation of Peace on 3 July 1919 from an armoured car outside the Town Hall. Large-scale civic celebrations were organized for 19

July, including a 'Monster Grand Procession', a 'Grand Fancy Dress Carnival, Parade and Battle of Flowers' and a 'Monster Beacon Bonfire' on the Common.

SIR ROBERT GOWER formally receives the tank presented to the town on 30 July 1919 by the National War Savings Committee. The tank had been brought in procession from the Goods Station to its final resting place on a grass verge here at the junction between London Road and Vale Road. Great excitement was caused en route by the tank making an unscheduled detour across the edge of the Common, scattering the spectators gathered there.

TUNBRIDGE WELLS BOROUGH FIRE BRIGADE, photographed with their one motor fire engine on 12 March 1921. Their Captain, Charles Prior, who was also Chief Constable of the Borough Police, stands in the front row, fourth from the right. The Brigade had been established in 1845 and it had its headquarters in Calverley Street, by the Town Hall.

THE UNVEILING OF THE WAR MEMORIAL at Mount Pleasant by Colonel Viscount Hardinge on 11 February 1923. The monument was dedicated by Archdeacon A.T. Scott and the Guard of Honour was furnished by the 4th Battalion of the Royal West Kent Regiment. This photograph was taken towards the end of the ceremony, following the Last Post and wreath laying by the mayor (Councillor Septimus Parsonage), the British Legion and others.

HAROLD CAMBURN PRODUCED SEVERAL VIEWS of the War Memorial taken shortly after the unveiling. Here passers-by stop to inspect the enormous array of floral tributes placed as the closing act of the ceremony by relatives and friends of those commemorated.

MEMBERS OF THE TUNBRIDGE WELLS BOROUGH POLICE photographed on 28 May 1915 with their Chief Constable, Charles Prior. The town had had its own police force since the institution of its first local government in 1835. The Police Station adjoined the Town Hall and had its entrance in Calverley Street.

THE OPENING OF THE CADOGAN PLAYING FIELD at St John's Road by Edward, Prince of Wales, on 25 July 1928. Immense excitement was generated by this brief and informal royal visit which began with the Prince's attendance at the Agricultural Show in Eridge Road. Cheering crowds lined the route from the show ground to St John's Road, where the Prince unlocked the gates of the Playing Field with a ceremonial golden key.

THE DUCHESS OF YORK, flanked by the Lord Lieutenant of Kent, the Marquis Camden, and the Bishop of Rochester, lays the foundation stone of the Kent and Sussex Hospital on 19 July 1932. The Hospital was built on the site of Decimus Burton's Great Culverden house to replace the old General Hospital in Grosvenor Road and the Ear and Eye Hospital on Mount Sion. The Kent and Sussex was opened by the Marchioness Camden on 25 July 1934.

ST JOHN'S CHURCH, one of a series of postcards showing illuminations to commemorate the Silver Jubilee of George V in 1935. The town's main celebrations were held on 6 May and included commemorative tree planting on the Common, a service of thanksgiving in Calverley Grounds, and a carnival procession.

THE ARMISTICE DAY SERVICE at the War Memorial on Friday 11 November 1938. The *Courier* records that 'as 11 o'clock struck, workmen standing high up on the scaffolding of the new Assembly Hall removed their caps and stood in silence; ... bus drivers stood beside their silent engines.' The mayor seen here, Alderman C.E. Westbrook, had taken up office just a few days previously and was to serve throughout the war until November 1945.

THE TUNBRIDGE WELLS BOROUGH SPECIAL CONSTABULARY photographed with Chief Constable Guy Carlton outside the new Town Hall building in 1941. The Police had already moved into their new headquarters around the corner in Crescent Road, but completion of other parts of the Civic Centre complex had been interrupted by the war. Guy Carlton served from 1927 until the amalgamation of the Borough force with the Kent County Constabulary in 1943.

GROSVENOR ROAD, VIEWED FROM FIVE WAYS, decorated for the coronation of Elizabeth II in 1953, in a photograph by R.J. Glass. The town's official programme of celebrations records events running from May to November. On coronation day itself, 2 June, the Higher Cricket Ground was the scene for a 'fancy dress parade, community singing, high wire act, broadcast of Queen's message, bands, bonfire and firework display'.

CAMDEN ROAD IN CORONATION YEAR, 1953, viewed from the junction with Calverley Road, again by Glass. On the right-hand corner is Decimus Burton's Camden Hotel, demolished in 1959 along with the old Town Hall. Its site and that of the adjoining shops is now occupied by the National Provident building of 1966.

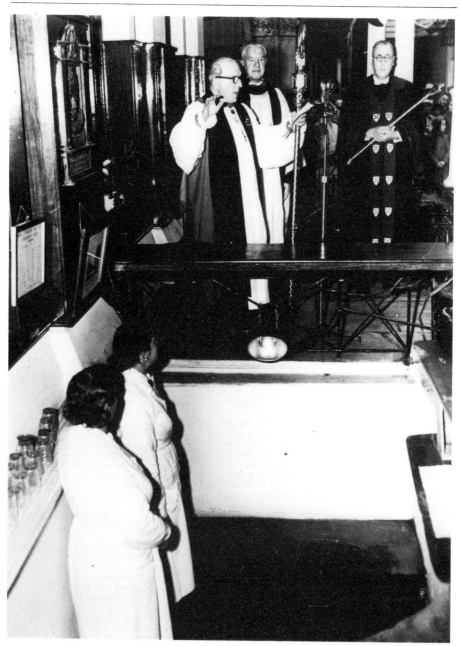

THE BISHOP OF ROCHESTER, DR C.M. CHAVASSE, blesses the chalybeate spring at the Pantiles on 7 September 1956. This followed a civic service of thanksgiving, led from the Pantiles bandstand, to celebrate the 350th anniversary of the discovery of the Tunbridge Wells waters in 1606 which led to the development of the town.

Streets and Buildings

THE NORTHERN APEX OF THE COMMON, bounded by Mount Ephraim (to the right) and London Road. Belleville, the cottage at the centre, has lost its half-timbering since this photograph was taken late in the 1800s. Built on a sandstone outcrop, the cottage has a cellar hewn out of the solid rock. Nearby are caves used for stabling donkeys, and later employed as air raid shelters during the Second World War.

ALONG MOUNT EPHRAIM, a little beyond Belleville, set back from the road, is the Mount Ephraim Hotel, later renamed the Royal Wells Inn. Built in 1834, the Hotel incorporated part of the old Hare and Hounds tavern. A town guide of 1892 recorded that 'among the influential classes the hotel is undoubtedly popular, and in situation, comfort, privacy and convenience it is surpassed by no contemporary concern.'

THE WELLINGTON HOTEL AND ROCKS, MOUNT EPHRAIM, from a postcard of c. 1900. This moonlit scene was contrived mainly in the photographer's darkroom. The Italianate Wellington opened in 1875 after the conversion of five private dwellings. The 1892 town guide notes the distinguished patronage by the Duke of Wellington. But, although his wife frequented Tunbridge Wells, the Duke was not known to have visited the town.

GIBRALTAR COTTAGE, situated at the Common apex, just below Belleville and St Helena. In the first half of the nineteenth century the Burrows family of Tunbridge ware manufacturers had factories here at Gibraltar, at the Parade and at Jordan House. The Cottage was built c.1828 and is attributed to Decimus Burton. His Holy Trinity Church is beyond.

A VIEW NORTH ALONG MOUNT EPHRAIM dating from the 1860s. Viewed from the left are Mansel House (now 42 Mount Ephraim), then and now housing the chemists Miller and Co.; No. 40, then called 1 Mount Ephraim Terrace, being the premises of fruiterer and greengrocer Stephen Starr; No. 38, then 2 Mount Ephraim Terrace, the drapery and furniture shop of George Spencer; and No. 36, or 3 Mount Ephraim Terrace, accommodating Frederick William Nye's pastry and confectionery business. Only the building at Nos 34 and 36 has changed substantially, having been rebuilt on a grander scale.

SALEM INDEPENDENT CHAPEL, St John's Road, was built in 1866 by the nonconformist evangelist Thomas Edwards. For two years from 1897 it became the St John's Free Church when Revd James Mountain, pastor of Emmanuel Church, found himself unable to comply with Article XIV of the Countess of Huntingdon's Connexion regarding infant baptism. Several members of Mountain's flock prevailed upon him not to leave town. Hence, the Free Church was formed. In 1935 the Chapel was purchased by the Maidstone and District bus company. Soon after which the building was razed to make way for a bus depot.

THE GENERAL HOSPITAL, GROSVENOR ROAD. The Dispensary of 1829 moved up to Grosvenor Road in 1842. The handsome original building can be seen to the left in this view. The Hospital was supported by voluntary contributions. Subscriptions and donations allowed enlargement in 1870 and 1884. Then in 1904 the extension stretching to Goods Station Road was opened. In 1934 the General Hospital moved to Mount Ephraim, becoming the Kent and Sussex Hospital. The entire block on Grosvenor Road was demolished and rebuilt as Five Ways Post Office and Coronation Parade in 1937.

CALVERLEY ROAD viewed from the west end. As it does today, the left side presented an assortment of buildings, from the grand Grosvenor Tavern to modest single storey lock-ups. Regular street markets were held along here at the beginning of this century. The entire block to the right was built in the 1870s by Charles Adie. Waymarks, drapers and furnishers, was opened by Ebenezer Waymark in 1875. Until its closure in 1958, the store was a local institution stocking high-class drapery and 'a constant succession of up-to-date novelties from the leading centres of fashion'.

CALVERLEY ROAD viewed from Five Ways junction, 26 May 1990. At first glance little has changed. The terrace by Adie seems to have survived unscathed. However, a large portion of it was rebuilt completely in 1989, resulting in a remarkably accurate copy of the original building. To the left, three large holes in the line of buildings are the result of demolitions for the Royal Victoria Place project. Halfway down the street the attractive facade of the Burton's building was dismantled and later reassembled several feet to the west in May to July 1991.

CAMDEN HOTEL and the Tunbridge Wells School of Arts and Crafts (occupying the former Town Hall) just before their demolition in 1959. The old Town Hall began life in 1835 as Calverley Market, part of Decimus Burton's Mount Pleasant development. The Town Commissioners took over the Market in 1858, and it remained the Town Hall until March 1941, when the Town Hall at the Civic Centre opened.

OBSCURED BY TREES to the left of this view along Mount Pleasant is Decimus Burton's Calverley Parade of 1834. The Calverley estate of about 900 acres had been acquired in 1825 by John Ward. Burton (1800–81) was retained by Ward to develop the western edge of this land as a new residential town. Thus was created in the 1830s a comprehensive development taking in a church, buildings for shops and businesses, hotels, a market place, cottages, large terraced residences and the grand villas of Calverley Park.

A SIMILAR VIEW OF MOUNT PLEASANT after widening of the roadway. The Parade can be seen as well as what is now the Lloyd's Bank building by H.H. Cronk, 1885.

MOUNT PLEASANT, LOOKING SOUTH, 26 May 1990. Calverley Parade has been replaced by the Civic Centre. The Town Hall stands to the right of the Library and Museum Building. Accompanying the usual displays of local history and archaeology, the Museum contains a fine collection of Tunbridge ware, the wooden souvenir ware made locally since the late seventeenth century.

MOUNT PLEASANT at the turn of the century, dominated by the Opera House of 1902. In the distance is the Grosvenor Tavern and Five Ways.

TUNBRIDGE WELLS. MONSON ST & CONGREGATIONAL CHAPEL.

MONSON ROAD viewed from the east, c.1905. To the left are the Public Baths. Behind is the Technical Institute designed by H.T. Hare, 1902. C.R.F. Lutwidge, twice mayor of the town, presented a stained glass window for the stairwell representing science, industry, art and commerce. Lord Avebury opened the Institute and 800 students were enrolled for full-time courses. The Institute continues as the Adult Education Centre. On the other side of the street is the Opera House block, while Monson Colonnade is to the right.

MONSON ROAD, TUNBRIDGE WELLS.
J.R.401.

MONSON COLONNADE (right) was erected in 1889 by local builder Henry Adams. There is no direct access between the shops and the dwellings above. The houses are approached via external stairs to the balcony which itself provides a covered area for the display of wares. Here, opposite the Colonnade, is the architecturally similar Monson Terrace (centre), missing just the balcony and ground-floor shops. At the right of this postcard from the early 1900s by J. Richards is Mr J. Haffenden's florist and nursery establishment. Monson Baths is behind.

AN AERIAL VIEW OF THE NEW CIVIC CENTRE COMPLEX, built after Calverley Parade and Calverley Terrace were demolished. In the centre is the massive Town Hall and Assembly Hall. Designed by Percy Thomas and Ernest Prestwich, the Assembly Hall was the first part to be opened, by the Marchioness Camden, on Empire Day 1939. The mayor, Cllr C.E. Westbrook, opened the Town Hall on 20 March 1941. Due to the intervention of the Second World War, the Library and Museum building (left) had to wait until 27 October 1952 for the opening by Lord De L'Isle and Dudley. To the right of the Assembly Hall is the Police Station, with one remnant of the Terrace beyond.

MOUNT PLEASANT CONGREGATIONAL CHURCH viewed from the Library and Museum building. Built in 1845–8, this typically nonconformist hall church was greatly improved by the addition of a grand Tuscan portico in 1866. Although the exterior is well preserved, the interior has been cleared and transformed into a shop (1981–3).

THE PRIORY AND HOLY TRINITY CHURCH. The church was built in the Perpendicular style by Burton as the new parish church for Tunbridge Wells on a site just off the Calverley estate. The foundation stone was laid on the birthday of the Duchess of Kent on 17 August 1827. In 1973 the church was declared redundant. Holy Trinity avoided demolition and went on to be the home of the Trinity Arts Centre. The Priory is a pair of large Tudor-style houses adjacent to the church, also by Burton.

LOOKING DOWN MOUNT PLEASANT ROAD in 1953, by Sydney Lazell. Classical details decorate the two terraces erected in the 1870s by Charles Adie. At the bottom is the Great Hall. Lazell produced many photographs for inclusion in official town guidebooks, although he was primarily a medical photographer who worked from a studio at No. 167 Upper Grosvenor Road.

GEORGE GLANVILLE'S PHOTOGRAPH of the Great Hall from an album of 1884. Designed by H.H. Cronk, and built 1870–2, the French Empire style dominates, although prominent classical columns and a pediment rose up over the main entrance. Intended to provide public rooms for entertainment, the building contained at various times a restaurant, club rooms, photographic studios, a cinema, a school of dancing and the hall itself, which was said to accommodate 1,200 people. In 1984 the Hall was subjected to a restoration and conversion. At the ground floor the central facade was rebuilt flush with the faces of the hitherto projecting wings, and the *porte-cochere* was reproduced in a scaled-down form. Some of the arguably out-of-place classical details were replaced by a French-style roof over the entrance that complements the ogee roofs of the wings. The main body received a bold mansard roof to accommodate offices, while the ground floor was converted to retail premises.

THE LOWER END OF MOUNT PLEASANT viewed from the High Street – the first of four views showing its development. This earliest view dates from about 1890. To the right, on the corner of Mount Pleasant Road and Grove Hill Road, is the Railway Bell Hotel. Just beyond is the then small shop of R.W. Weekes, opened in 1854. Across the road is the Central Station. A painted advertisement states, 'Special Cheap Return Tickets to London on Wednesdays 10s 7s 3s6d'.

IN 1907 THE SOUTH EASTERN AND CHATHAM RAILWAY COMPANY rebuilt the railway bridge of 1851. The mayor, Cllr B.M. Woollan, opened the widened bridge on 16 May shortly before this photograph was taken. In the centre of this view and to the left is the Central Station, erected 1845–6. Here the upside building is in the midst of alteration. Since the last photograph, the three buildings north of the hotel have grown to dominate the bottom of the hill.

A NEW, GRAND, DOWNSIDE BUILDING FOR CENTRAL STATION was designed by A.W. Blomfield and opened in 1912. To the right, not visible in this view, Messrs Weekes had in 1911 continued their conquest of the bottom of Mount Pleasant by purchasing and demolishing the Railway Bell Hotel. They erected a building on the corner vaguely in harmony with their existing premises.

MOUNT PLEASANT, 26 May 1990. At first glance little has changed in seventy years. To the left, the once dominant tower of Holy Trinity Church is obscured by a massive block possessing debatable architectural merit. At the centre, three huge cranes assist in the construction of the 300,000 sq ft Royal Victoria Place development. Much of Weekes has been rebuilt, and, later in 1990, new owners abandoned the name Weekes in favour of Hoopers.

HIGH STREET, looking south from the railway bridge in about 1906. Some of the buildings at this end were altered when the bridge was rebuilt and the road widened. To the left is the

castellated tower of Christ Church, which was built in 1835–41 in a neo-Norman style to designs by R. Palmer Brown. Edward Burne-Jones designed the stained glass of 1878.

ST JAMES' CHURCH, SAINT JAMES ROAD. Built 1860–2 from a design by Ewan Christian in the Decorated gothic style. The church was built of sandstone, costing £6,000. The north aisle was added in 1883, along with a vestry by J. Oldrid Scott.

SKINNERS' SCHOOL, ST JOHN'S ROAD, viewed from the playing fields. Built in red brick Tudor style, the school opened in September 1877 after much controversy. Following the Endowed Schools Act, The Skinners' Company offered to build a middle-grade school in or near Tonbridge. Since Tonbridge already had a grammar school, Tunbridge Wells vied with Tonbridge for the second establishment. Both towns won. A year after Tunbridge Wells opened its Skinners' School, Tonbridge opened the Judd Commercial School.

LITTLE MOUNT SION, photographed by D.J. Johnson on 19 September 1934. After the Restoration, Mount Sion grew in popularity and soon rivalled Mount Ephraim. A 'village' grew up there close to the Wells, with some buildings actually transported to the site. Thomas Benge Burr, writing in 1766, states that 'many houses were brought from Southborough, Rusthall, and Mount-Ephraim, to be rebuilt on Mount-Sion; and some, whole and entire as they were, were wheeled on sledges to be fixed in this new seat of favour.'

ROCK VIEW, dating from the late eighteenth or early nineteenth century, at the corner of Dudley Road and London Road, photographed by Johnson in 1921. The Victoria Hotel, at the left, was renamed the Russell in about 1924.

ROYAL TUNBRIDGE WELLS viewed from Mount Ephraim in the 1950s. Gibraltar Cottage overlooks London Road. At the near end of Church Road stands Jordan House, a residence and shop for the Tunbridge ware manufacturers Humphrey Burrows Snr and Jnr from about 1800 until 1845. Church Road passes Holy Trinity Church, and at the far end is the Civic Centre.

LONDON ROAD VIEWED FROM THE COMMON. The tower of Christ Church looms over the High Street, and in the background is the Grove on Mount Sion. At the far right is Vale Royal Methodist Church. In the 1770s and 1780s John Wesley preached at Tunbridge Wells on a number of occasions. Of his visit on 19 January 1778 he wrote that he 'preached in the large Dissenting Meeting-house to a numerous congregation, and deep attention sat on every face.' The first chapel at Vale Royal opened on 24 June 1812. This made way for the present building in 1872, opened 2 June 1873.

THE ARCHITECTURALLY BARREN SIDE of the main post office which faces London Road. When opened in 1896, the mayor, Major Lutwidge, pointed out that the building seems to face the wrong way, with its attractive facade on narrow Vale Road rather than facing across an expanse of lawn and London Road. In front is the tank seen on p. 20.

THE ROYAL KENTISH HOTEL, photographed by D. Everest before the rebuilding of 1878. J. Clifford wrote in 1823 that the hotel 'has lately undergone great improvements, which have amply repaid the proprietor for his exertions.' Along with the Royal Sussex Hotel on the Pantiles, the Royal Kentish was the starting point for frequent coaches to London, Hastings, Brighton and the Medway towns.

D.J. JOHNSON'S 1934 VIEW of the bottom of London Road. The imposing building in the centre was the new Royal Kentish Hotel. Completely rebuilt in 1878, the building incorporated a passenger lift, speaking tubes, an immense kitchen, and for some years it was the tallest building in the town. After being called the Grand Hotel earlier in this century, the building later became the residential Kentish Mansions.

LOOKING NORTH from the bottom of London Road, probably in the 1860s. The Church of King Charles the Martyr is to the right, outside of this view, and the Royal Kentish Hotel is obscured by the waggons. In the distance can be seen the four fine poplar trees, said to be among the first of their kind in Kent, which stood outside the first Vale Royal Methodist Church until its replacement by the present building in 1872–3.

THE JUNCTION OF CHAPEL PLACE and Mount Sion Road photographed shortly after the rebuilding of the Royal Kentish Hotel in 1878.

JOHNSON'S VIEW OF THE CHURCH OF KING CHARLES THE MARTYR in 1926. Thomas Benge Burr wrote in 1766 that the young Tunbridge Wells became a populous and flourishing village, and 'the piety of our ancestors made them think it necessary to build an house to the honour of God'. Thus, in 1676 a subscription was opened to raise a fund for building a chapel. The chapel was built on land given by Viscountess Purbeck of Summerhill and it first opened for worship in 1678. Pious inhabitants soon overwhelmed the church, and by 1696 the building had almost doubled in size in order to accommodate the faithful.

THE INTERIOR OF KING CHARLES CHURCH, again by Johnson in 1926. The most striking feature is the ornate plaster ceiling, designed and begun by John Wetherell in 1678 and completed after 1690 by Henry Doogood. Their work forms a series of low domes outlined by wreaths of fruit and garlands, with winged heads of putti and palm leaves filling the interstices. The unusual symmetry of the ceiling is a result of the church's ritual east end, the site of the altar, changing orientation as the chapel grew. The section of ceiling visible in this view is that of the earlier church, and it shows the original orientation with the 'east end' actually facing north-east (left). Enlargement of the church, and the addition of the chancel in 1882, led to an altar at the south-east.

D.J. JOHNSON'S VIEW across Nevill Street into the Pantiles, the site of Tunbridge Wells's premier chalybeate spring. Dudley, Lord North (1581–1666), discovered the spring in 1606 while returning to London from Lord Abergavenny's seat at Eridge. He noticed the scummy waters of a stream within the Waterdown Forest and recognized a similarity to the medicinal waters at Spa. Tests were ordered, and their results led eventually to claims by physicians that the waters had health-restoring properties.

BATH SQUARE, THE PANTILES, at the turn of the century. Initially the chalybeate spring was enclosed by modest wooden palings. Celia Fiennes (1697) and Burr (1766) give detailed descriptions of the triangular stone enclosure built by the Lord of the Manor, Viscount Muskerry, in 1664 and the two 'large basons of stone fixt in the earth with severall holes in the bottom by which the springs bubble up and fill it'. At the centre of this photograph is the Bath House, erected directly behind the spring in 1803–5. The portico over the well was added in 1847 after a public subscription.

THE ACCOMMODATION OF THE NEW BATH HOUSE boasted vapour, shower and ordinary hot and cold baths, it being considered healthy to bathe in as well as to drink the water. Behind the spring is this cold plunging bath, still preserved in the cellar of the Bath House, which was abolished during the improvements of 1847. The bath was filled by the surplus water running from the chalybeate spring. As the iron rapidly precipitates from the water, according to Pelton, 'you generally plunged into a stagnant, turbid, rusty pool, and emerged in a condition very much resembling a hide from a tanner's yard'.

THE CORN EXCHANGE AND THE MUSICK GALLERY in about 1889. Although a plaque on the Gallery states that it is the original structure, several drawings from the later 1700s depict clearly a sturdy wooden building. This earlier Gallery was free-standing among the trees in front of the adjoining building which was then the Gloster Tavern. The Corn Exchange, with a statue of Ceres complete with scythe and cornucopia standing over the facade, was built as a theatre by Sarah Baker in 1802. Today, shops and the A Day at the Wells heritage centre are found within.

LOOKING SOUTH ALONG THE PANTILES from Bath Square in around 1905. The Pantiles is named after the paving once employed here. At other times it has been called the Walks and the Parade, or the Royal Parade. Visits by Queen Henrietta Maria in 1630, and Dr Rowzee's praise of the waters in his book *The Queen's Wells*, were followed by increasing numbers of visitors to the Wells and increasing need for accommodation and services. In the later 1630s the Walks began to develop, complete with lodging houses, a coffee house and tradesmen's stalls.

LOOKING SOUTH ALONG THE PANTILES, 26 May 1990. Association of pantiles with the Pantiles began in 1700. Princess Anne donated £100 in 1698 for new paving on the Upper Walk after her son, the Duke of Gloucester, had fallen on the slippery ground. The square clay tiling was laid in diagonal rows over the Upper Walk in 1700. This surface lasted until 1793 when pantiles were replaced by the now familiar stone flags. The last remaining pantiles, in Bath Square, were conserved at the British Museum in 1990 and then deposited at Tunbridge Wells Museum.

OTHER THAN THE PAVING, the colonnade to the west is the most unusual feature of the Pantiles. The sheltered walkway is supported mostly on Tuscan columns of varying dates. The thin, plain columns to the left of this photograph (c.1890) are among the oldest. Behind the colonnade are buildings of numerous dates and styles. Although seventeenth- and eighteenth-century structures hide underneath, many of these buildings received new facades and were raised to grander proportions in the late 1800s. But several buildings of around 1800 and earlier can be seen, low, weather-boarded, and modest.

PUMP ROOM, TUNBRIDGE WELLS

THE PUMP ROOM, built 1877–8 at the opposite end of the Pantiles to the Bath House. Soon after its completion an article in the *Illustrated London News* noted that it was 'designed for the convenience of visitors attending the daily administration of the medicinal draught, a boon of kind Nature to the invalid or debilitated, but here made of easier and more agreeable reception by the artificial provision of many suitable comforts.' The building was demolished in 1964, to be replaced by the Union House shop and office development.

BRIGHTON STATION, later known as West Station, in Montacute Road, was built in 1866 after a design by C.H. Driver when the London, Brighton and South Coast railway company extended their line from East Grinstead. Here travellers enjoyed 'very commodious waiting rooms and offices, with a broad covered platform, 1,125 feet in length'. After closure by British Rail, the Tunbridge Wells and Eridge Railway Preservation Society drew up plans to open a private line from the station to Eridge named the Spa Valley Railway. In 1990 the main station building became a restaurant.

Open Spaces

THE NORTHERN SECTION OF TUNBRIDGE WELLS COMMON, showing the sweep of London Road at the centre and Mount Ephraim on the horizon to the left. On London Road at the far right is the original Vale Royal with Romanoff Cottage adjoining to the left. Both of these were demolished to make way for what is now the Vale Royal Hotel, built in 1898 as a terrace of private houses. The Common forms part of the Manor of Rusthall and the first guarantee against encroachment came in the Rusthall Manor Act of 1739.

37055. Tunbridge Wells. The Common .P.C.

IN VICTORIAN AND EDWARDIAN TIMES the Common was a very popular resort, and several postcards of the period depict the crowds that gathered there on Sunday afternoons. This view, from about 1905, shows crowds on the slopes overlooking London Road. Contemporary guides declared that 'what the ocean is to a sea-bathing town, that the Common is to Tunbridge Wells', and gave eloquent descriptions of the beauties of the gorse, heather, bracken and other wild plants.

BETWEEN 1962 AND 1964 the photographer, artist and natural historian Harold Betteridge (1892–1972), a well-known local eccentric, compiled two albums of photographs entitled 'A Practical Appreciation of Tunbridge Wells Common', depicting its scenery in different seasons. Included is this winter scene looking towards London Road, with the junction with Church Road to the right.

AN EXTENSIVE PANORAMA OF THE COMMON on a postcard published about 1908, showing at the centre the Lower Cricket Ground, levelled in 1885. Castle Road runs across the picture. At this period the Common was still extensively grazed by sheep and cattle which prevented the growth of trees and preserved its character as open heathland. The cessation of grazing later in the century has led to a process of reversion to woodland which a recently-begun management programme seeks to arrest.

THE COTTAGE, a picturesque but little-known building, stands in an obscure location on the western boundary of the Common. Generally ignored by local guides and postcard publishers, it was not overlooked by Betteridge in his 1960s series of views of the Common. The Cottage was the summer retreat from about 1850 of the Scottish preacher and controversialist Revd Dr John Cumming (1807–81), and his daughters, Ethel and Lettice, lived in the Cottage until quite recently.

A DELIGHTFUL PERIOD PIECE from Betteridge's album. Three schoolgirls are sketching Gibraltar Cottage, the southernmost of the three houses built onto sandstone outcrops on the apex of the Common. The middle cottage, St Helena, is obscured by trees in the background.

ALTHOUGH FED BY A NATURAL SPRING, Brighton Lake, at the southern edge of the Common, is a largely artificial construction excavated for the use of children in 1858. The project was inspired by William Law Pope, the popular minister of King Charles' Church from 1829 to 1879, to provide work for the town's unemployed. Costs were met by a public appeal. This view dating from about 1903 features some of the sheep which grazed the Common well into the present century.

ROMANOFF LODGE, CASTLE ROAD, the Common, photographed about 1918 by Harold Camburn. At this period it was a private hotel, the Romanoff Pension. It was built in 1852 by Thomas R. Allfree, proprietor of Romanoff House, a private boarding school in London Road which he founded in the 1830s. Allfree had been a tutor to the Russian royal family and named his establishment accordingly.

MOUNT EDGECOMBE ROCKS on the northern edge of the Common, where Church Road meets Mount Ephraim, were well known in Victorian and Edwardian times and they were often depicted on postcards and in local guides. They provided a popular vantage point for views over the town, appearing in the foreground of numerous published illustrations. The Rocks have since fallen into obscurity through becoming overgrown.

'SATURDAY AFTERNOON ON THE ROCKS' by Harold Betteridge well illustrates the continuing popularity as a children's playground of Wellington Rocks, the most prominent of the sandstone outcrops on the Common. They were named after the nearby Wellington Hotel, which opened in 1875. An engraving of 1863 describes them as the 'High Rocks, Mount Ephraim' and shows them being climbed not by children but by fashionable adult visitors.

CALVERLEY GROUNDS, pictured here in the early 1950s by Sydney Lazell, was originally the private grounds of the Calverley Hotel (visible at the top of the picture). It was purchased by the Council in 1920 for use as a public park, and a programme of improvements commenced. These included the laying out of the rose garden in the foreground, the building of the originally thatched tea-house, and the construction of tennis courts and a bowling green.

THE BURMESE BELL in the rose garden in Calverley Grounds was given to the town about 1933 by descendants of Sir Edward Sladen (1827–90). Sladen was appointed in 1864 as the British government's representative to the court of King Mindon of Burma, who in 1866 awarded him the country's order of knighthood as a result of assistance rendered during a rebellion. When in 1869 Sladen had the bell cast, he met with opposition, since bells were employed only for religious purposes, but the king intervened in his favour.

LAZELL'S PHOTOGRAPH of the small bank near the Mount Pleasant entrance of Calverley Grounds which was used until about 1985 for regularly changing floral displays. Some displays were purely decorative, while others commemorated local organizations and national or civic events, such as this design for the coronation of 1953. The site is now occupied by a memorial, erected in 1987, to Air Chief Marshal Lord Dowding, Commander-in-Chief of Fighter Command during the Battle of Britain, who spent his retirement in the town.

THE PAVILION AND BANDSTAND in Calverley Grounds soon after their opening in 1926. The pavilion provided covered seating for an audience of up to 1,200, while an equal number could sit in the open around the stand. It was gutted by an incendiary bomb on 26 September 1940 and was never rebuilt. The bandstand survived the fire and remained in use though losing much of its ornate ironwork.

THE GROVE, pictured here in about 1910, was given to the town by the self-styled Earl of Buckingham to be preserved as an open space under the care of a board of trustees. In later years it suffered neglect but was tidied and replanted in the 1860s through the efforts of Revd W.L. Pope. In 1890 it was taken over by the Council who in 1897 erected a bandstand so that concerts could be held in the summer months.

'CAROLLING', SET ON RUSTHALL COMMON, was exhibited by Tunbridge Wells photographer Henry Peach Robinson at the Photographic Society of Great Britain in 1887. Although successfully appearing natural and spontaneous, the picture is in fact carefully composed from four

negatives and it is based upon an initial pencil sketch. Robinson found that real country folk did not take kindly to being posed and photographed, so for his figures he often employed members of his family and friends in costume.

Toad Rock, Rusthall, Royal Tunbridge Wells.

AN UNUSUAL VIEW OF TOAD ROCK in its context of the 'village' of Denny Bottom, produced about 1913 by Harold Camburn for Agnes Kemp, proprietor of the local store and post office at the right of this picture. In the background are orchards which were built over in the 1930s. The Toad first appears in local guides in the early nineteenth century when it is described as being surrounded by 'broken ground, pig-sties, rude cottages, and small enclosures'.

IN ADDITION TO HIS ALBUMS illustrating Tunbridge Wells Common, Harold Betteridge compiled at about the same time a similar collection of views of Rusthall Common, including this picture of rocks at Denny Bottom near Toad Rock. The entrance to Rusthall Park is in the background.

IN VICTORIAN AND EDWARDIAN TIMES the Toad was only the most prominent of a cluster of named rock formations which were pointed out to visitors. These included the Parson's Nose, the Elephant, the Lion, the Pig's Head, the Pulpit, and the Cradle. Since apparently they were never mapped or illustrated, most of these cannot now be identified. One which can still be spotted is the Loaf Rock, although it often escapes notice through being tucked away by the cottages in Upper Street. This view dates from about 1912.

IN THE FIRST QUARTER OF THE PRESENT CENTURY Bull's Hollow, an isolated corner of Rusthall Common, enjoyed a brief spell of popularity as a beauty spot, being illustrated regularly in the official town guides, for which this picture was taken in 1940. The site is a former quarry, said to be named after a quarryman who lived and worked there. Now little known to tourists, the rocks remain popular with climbers.

A PANORAMIC VIEW OF THE HAPPY VALLEY in 1873 by George Glanville, a local professional photographer whose work is prominent in late Victorian albums and guides. The Valley seems not to have come into prominence as a beauty spot much before the date of this picture. Although now the name applies to the southern section of Rusthall Common, it then referred to a wider area covering private grounds further south where the Cold Bath of 1708 could still be seen.

EDWARDIAN VISITORS TO THE HAPPY VALLEY, decribed in an official town guide of the period as 'a charming place to which neither pen nor picture can do really adequate justice'. The eighteenth-century flight of stone steps which formerly led down to the Cold Bath are still visible. Other cold baths of similar date survive at the Pantiles, Fonthill and Langton Green.

THE FORMER HIGH ROCKS FARM near the junction of Tea Garden Lane with High Rocks Lane, as shown in the town guide of 1940. The view is taken as it would be seen by walkers along the recommended route to the High Rocks from Tunbridge Wells Common. The separate farm buildings have subsequently been converted into individual dwellings.

THE VICTORIAN ENTRANCE TO THE HIGH ROCKS in about 1905. The Rocks are said to have been first popularized by the Duke of York (later James II), who visited them in 1670. They were enclosed in the early nineteenth century and became part of the grounds of the present High Rocks Inn (formerly the Cape of Good Hope), built in 1839 but replacing an earlier structure. The entrance fee of sixpence had remained static since at least 1840.

A POPULAR EDWARDIAN VIEW OF THE HIGH ROCKS showing one of several footbridges over chasms. Such embellishments were added and maintained over the years by successive proprietors of the High Rocks Inn. Excavations from 1954 to 1961 revealed that the remarkable sandstone cliffs with their overhangs had been used as shelters by Middle Stone Age hunters and later as natural defences for an Iron Age hill-fort.

A SECOND EDWARDIAN VIEW OF THE HIGH ROCKS shows on the left the verses inscribed by local publisher and bookseller James Phippen.

> Infidel! who, with thy finite wisdom,
> Wouldst grasp things Infinite, and dost become,
> A scoffer of God's holiest Mysteries,
> Behold this Rock, then tremble and rejoice:
> Tremble! for He who form'd the mighty mass,
> Could, in His Justice, crush thee where thou art;
> Rejoice! – that still His Mercy spares thee.
> March 21st 1831   J. Phippen

At the centre of this view a sign points to the Bell Rock, which is approached through a narrow chasm. According to nineteenth-century guides, the Bell Rock emitted a 'strange metallic sound' when struck, clubs being provided by the proprietor for the purpose. The ringing is referred to in guides as late as the 1930s. But in a 1964 booklet on the Rocks the then proprietor admitted that the Bell had ceased to sound.

GROSVENOR RECREATION GROUND was opened in 1889 on the site of the town dust heap and redundant waterworks, with additional land donated by John Stone-Wigg. In addition to the lake surviving today, the park originally contained an open-air swimming pool and the ornamental ponds depicted on this postcard, published about 1908. The adjoining Hilbert Recreation Ground was presented to the town by Cllr E.J. Strange in 1930.

DUNORLAN, COMPLETED IN 1862, was built on the site of Calverley Manor Farm by the Tasmanian businessman and evangelist Henry Reed, an associate of William Booth, founder of the Salvation Army. Reed also landscaped the surrounding park. In the 1940s the estate was sold to the Council, who opened the grounds as a public park but could do nothing with the house, which was requisitioned and occupied from 1943 by the War Damage Commission. When the house was handed over finally in 1958, no alternative could be found but to demolish the property and to sell the site for development.

THE ROSERY, DUNORLAN, in about 1905, on a postcard published by James Richard of Camden Road. This part of the estate was laid out by Henry Reed as an avenue of conifers ornamented with statues leading from a Grecian temple to a stone basin with ornate fountain. Although the temple and fountain survive, the latter in an incomplete state, the statues were largely destroyed. This destruction is said to have been due to target practice by troops billeted in the house before the War Damage Commission took possession.

THE LAKE IN DUNORLAN PARK was constructed by Henry Reed on the site of an existing stream and pond. The sale brochure of 1872 describes it as a 'fine ornamental sheet of water of about six acres with prettily shaped islands and well stocked with fish'. Boating was introduced by the Council in about 1950 and was organized by the Matchett family, who also built a café in the park. This view was taken in the summer of 1959.

Sports and Entertainments

SPECTATORS BY THE PAVILION of the Higher Cricket Ground on the Common in about 1938. Cricket has been played on this site since the mid-eighteenth century. From 1845 until 1880 County matches were played here, but these ceased due to the poor condition of the pitch which was regularly trampled by the public and grazing animals. County matches only returned to the town in 1901 after the old ground had been superseded as the town's chief cricketing venue by the new Nevill Ground, opened in 1898.

A VIEW OF A MATCH in progress on the Higher Cricket Ground produced for the town guide of 1956. At this period the Ground was, as it is today, the home of the Linden Park Cricket Club, founded in 1876. It had originally been shared with two other clubs, the Tunbridge Wells Cricket Club, which traces its history back to the late eighteenth century, and the Blue Mantles, established in 1864; but these transferred their headquarters to the Nevill Ground in 1898.

SYDNEY LAZELL'S VIEW of Southborough Cricket Ground in about 1950. The Ground is the home of Southborough Cricket Club, which in 1938 celebrated the centenary of its earliest recorded match. In the background is the parish church of St Peter, built by Decimus Burton in 1830–1, with the west tower and spire added in 1883.

GOLFERS ON THE NEVILL COURSE, an illustration for the town guide of 1939. The Nevill Golf Club, founded in 1914, was the youngest of three active at this period. At the outbreak of the First World War, the construction of the course was interrupted with only nine holes completed, but subsequently the number was brought up to eighteen. The town's oldest course was opened by the Tunbridge Wells Golf Club near the Spa Hotel in 1890. The third club, the Culverden (founded 1896), had a course off Culverden Road, but this closed about 1950.

THE VALE RANGERS FOOTBALL CLUB team for the season 1899–1900. At this period the Rangers were one of some seventeen junior teams which in April 1899 had formed the Tunbridge Wells and District Football League. Their home ground was the Lower Cricket Ground. In June 1903 they achieved senior status, changed their name to Tunbridge Wells Rangers, and secured a new ground at Culverden Down. During the following season they adopted professionalism. The club flourished until the beginning of the Second World War.

BEFORE THE RANGERS turned professional, the amateur Tunbridge Wells Football Club (seen here in the 1907–8 season) had been the town's premier team. The two met for the first time in their new roles on 17 September 1904 when the result was a victory for the Rangers. At the time of this picture, the town club had recently returned to their old ground at Down Lane after a move in 1898 to the new Nevill Ground. By 1912 they had moved again, this time to Charity Farm, Ferndale (now the Hilbert Recreation Ground).

THE WATER POLO TEAM of the Cygnus Swimming Club which won the all-England cham-
pionship at Leicester on 9 October 1893. When the team returned to Tunbridge Wells on
the following day, they were met at the West Station by a torchlight procession headed by
the town band, which escorted them to the Great Hall. The club was founded in 1882 and
was supported by many local dignitaries including John Stone-Wigg, who served as
President until his death in 1897.

'FOR DOWNRIGHT ENJOYMENT and exhilarating fun there are few things that will compare with
the comic swimming race depicted here', wrote Albert Broadwell in an article for *The Strand
Magazine* in 1900. The race, in which competitors had successively to pick up hat, trousers,
coat and umbrella from different points along the pool side, was invented by the Cygnus
Swimming Club's secretary, W. Tyrrell Biggs, who arranged a special demonstration for the
author and accompanying photographer. The scene is the open air pool at Grosvenor
Recreation Ground.

THE INDOOR SWIMMING POOL IN MONSON ROAD, seen here in the late 1930s, was constructed by the Council to celebrate Queen Victoria's Diamond Jubilee. The Cygnus Swimming Club had compaigned actively for such a facility since an earlier covered pool was closed in 1888. It underwent improvements over the years, and in the 1950s could still be described as 'unmatchable in cleanliness, service and civility, and all necessary facilities'.

DESPITE THE OPENING OF THE MONSON BATHS, the open-air bath in Grosvenor Recreation Ground (opened in 1873 and pictured here by Lazell about 1939) remained popular and continued in use until 1948. At eighty-eight yards in length, it was once claimed to be the largest open-air pool in the south of England. The pool was originally a reservoir belonging to the Calverley Water Works Company and was fed by Jack Wood Spring, first tapped by John Ward to provide water for his new Calverley Estate.

THE GROSVENOR BOWLING CLUB'S GREEN is declared formally open for the new season by their President, Sir Robert Gower, on 16 May 1925. The Club, founded in 1913, was one of four in the town at this date. The two oldest, the Grove (established 1908) and the Tunbridge Wells (in St John's Road) had private greens, while the Grosvenor and Culverden clubs played on public greens in Grosvenor and St John's Recreation Grounds, respectively. A fifth club based at Calverley Grounds was soon to be formed.

'OF PARAMOUNT IMPORTANCE', says the 1939 town guide, 'is of course the Tunbridge Wells Bowling Tournament which since its inception in 1929 has made phenomenal strides. In addition to a large number of local players this tournament attracts exponents of international repute who have not been backward in their praise for the facilities which the town provides.' This Tournament week scene for the 1947 town guide shows the Grove Bowling Club's green off Grove Hill Gardens.

A SCENE AT THE ANNUAL OPEN LAWN TENNIS TOURNAMENT at the Nevill Ground in the late 1940s. The first tournament was held there in 1908, and the event has continued to the present day. When the Nevill Ground was first opened in 1898 football was played on the lower part of the site, but this proved unsuccessful, and in 1905 the area was taken over by the Tunbridge Wells Lawn Tennis Club.

CLIMBERS ON THE FACE OF THE OLD QUARRY at Bull's Hollow, Rusthall Common, photographed by Harold Betteridge between 1962 and 1964. Serious climbing of the sandstone outcrops of Tunbridge Wells began at High Rocks in the 1920s. The possibilities for climbers at Bull's Hollow were first publicized in 1947, and there are currently sixty-one named and listed routes at this site.

WORKMEN INVOLVED IN THE CONSTRUCTION OF THE OPERA HOUSE, the town's new theatre, in 1902. It was erected by local builder John Jarvis to designs by John Briggs, a London architect, on the site of two private houses, Monson Place and Monson House. The foundation stones were laid on 10 October 1901 by the actor Herbert Beerbohm Tree, the mayor (Alderman W.H. Delves), and Frederick Horner MP, the chairman of the Opera House Company.

Opera House, Tunbridge Wells.

THE OPERA HOUSE DEVELOPMENT incorporating shops and two banks, on a postcard of about 1908. The theatre was opened on 16 October 1902 with a performance of *Liberty Hall*, a comedy by R.C. Carton, followed by a specially written epilogue entitled *In Dr Johnson's Days*, set on the Pantiles in the 1740s when Beau Nash was Master of Ceremonies. The figure of Mercury, which can be seen on the central dome, was removed in the 1920s for reasons that remain obscure. Subsequently, it became lost.

'THE OPERA HOUSE ... is a very elegant theatre and decorated and fitted with great taste, and in quite the modern up-to-date style', declared Pelton's guide in 1905. The interior was designed in the style of Louis XV, and the 1,100 seats upholstered in crimson plush. In 1931 the theatre was converted into a cinema but continued to be used for some stage performances. In February 1968, amid much controversy, it closed to re-open six months later as a bingo hall.

'HIGH CLASS LONDON COMPANIES make flying matinée visits to this theatre', continues the 1905 guide, 'and the management provides a constant succession of modern theatrical performances given by the best touring companies that are seen out of London.' This photograph depicts a scene from *The New Barmaid*, a musical comedy staged in June of that year. The show's most popular song included additional 'local verses about the new South Eastern Bridge [recently the old railway bridge at the foot of Mount Pleasant had been declared unsafe] and other topics of the moment'.

'PLAYING ON THE PANTILES is no novelty to members of the Drama Club, who take great pleasure in acting in the works of our national poet in the sort of conditions that Shakespeare himself intended', according to a magazine article of 1959. Tunbridge Wells Drama Club was founded in 1946, and from 1951 it performed Shakespeare's plays annually on an open air stage in front of the Pantiles bandstand. This picture shows a scene from *The Merry Wives of Windsor*, their first production at this venue.

THE TUNBRIDGE WELLS BOROUGH BAND in their scarlet and white uniform, with conductor M. Marks. This group dates from 1896. In 1886 the band accepted an engagement to provide music for a world cruise on the SS *Ceylon*, from which it acquired the alternative name of the Ceylon Band. In the late 1920s the band went into decline and was reduced finally to a solitary cornet player (George Ellis, seen here third from the left in the back row) 'whose somewhat melancholy solos, in weather fair, foul or cold, only ceased when, poor man, he could no longer play'.

ROUGHLY CONTEMPORARY with the above group is this view of the Borough Band in action on the Pantiles, where they played five days a week from May to September in the mornings and alternate evenings. In the event of bad weather they played in the Pump Room. On the other evenings they performed at different venues including the Common, Calverley Park and Grosvenor Recreation Ground.

A CONCERT AT THE PANTILES BANDSTAND in 1952. The demise of the Borough Band in the 1920s did not mean the end of concerts on the Pantiles since a Corporation Band Committee had been established some years earlier to engage 'high class military and orchestral bands' to perform in the town. Despite a long history of Pantiles musical performances, the bandstand was not erected until 1900. Opened on 13 September of that year, it survived until 1969.

THE PANTILES BANDSTAND was the third to be constructed in the town, closely following those in the Grove (1897) and Grosvenor Recreation Ground (1899). The latter two, however, fell into disuse after the opening in 1926 of the bandstand and pavilion in Calverley Grounds, pictured here by Lazell in the early 1950s. At that time a temporary marquee took the place of the pavilion destroyed by a bomb in 1940.

People and Events

AMBROTYPE PORTRAIT OF THOMAS SIMS, a pioneer photographer who spent the latter part of his life in Tunbridge Wells. Born in Swansea in 1826, he was one of the first generation of professional photographers in Britain, setting up in business in Weston-super-Mare in 1847. In 1852 Sims exhibited examples of his work at Britain's first photographic exhibition, organized in London by the Society of Arts.

UNFORTUNATELY, THE LOCATION OF THIS DELIGHTFUL STUDY of a group of estate workers, taken by Thomas Sims in the 1860s, is unknown. Having established his reputation, Sims moved to London in 1853 where he soon had two separate studios. In 1868 he moved to Tunbridge Wells, working first in St John's Road and later in Grosvenor Road. He remained there as a professional photographer until his death in 1910.

DONKEY BOYS ON TUNBRIDGE WELLS COMMON, portrayed by Percy Lankester for *A Pictorial History of Tunbridge Wells*, published in 1892. The accompanying text states that 'visitors ... can even now have the opportunity of enjoying a donkey ride on the breezy heath'. Donkey riding is said to have been introduced to the town as a fashionable pastime in 1801 and was enjoyed by the young Princess Victoria on her visits in the late 1820s and 1830s.

A DIPPER AT THE CHALYBEATE SPRING in about 1860. These women were traditionally appointed by the Lord of the Manor of Rusthall to clean the spring basins and to dispense the waters to visitors. At this period the charge was a penny per glass, but those taking a course of the waters for medicinal purposes could save money by paying a subscription. The first dipper, Mrs Humphreys, was the local cottager who lent a wooden bowl to Lord North when he discovered the spring. She continued in office until her death in 1678 at the age of 102 years.

PRIOR TO 1865 THE TOWN'S WATER was supplied by two private companies, the Calverley and Tunbridge Wells Water Works Companies. In that year these were bought out by the Local Board which proceeded to excavate a new reservoir at Pembury. This soon proved inadequate when water shortages occurred in the dry summers of the 1880s, and work began on an extension. This picture by George Glanville, dated 30 April 1884, shows the engine house. The view is one of a series documenting this second period of excavation. The work was completed in 1886.

LOCAL PHOTOGRAPHER HENRY PEACH ROBINSON pictured in 1890 in the study of his home, Winwood, in Queens Road, by his son Ralph Winwood Robinson. Born in 1830, Robinson was a pioneer in the development of photography as an art form. While making a living as a conventional portrait photographer, Robinson specialized in the production of composite prints which allowed an effect analogous to the composition and style of paintings and drawings. He came to Tunbridge Wells in 1868, setting up a studio in Upper Grosvenor Road. In 1871 he acquired premises in the newly opened Great Hall, where he worked until his retirement in 1888. Robinson remained active in the photographic world until shortly before his death in 1901.

MEMBERS OF THE TUNBRIDGE WELLS AMATEUR PHOTOGRAPHIC ASSOCIATION at the ruins of Scotney Castle during an outing in 1890. The Association was founded in 1887 as a result of a lecture given at the Literary Society's rooms in the previous autumn by Ralph Winwood Robinson. He and his father were both founder members, and Sir David Salomons accepted a request to become the Association's patron, remaining an active supporter until his death in 1925. Later renamed the Royal Tunbridge Wells Photographic Society, the group remains active.

BRENTON HALLIBURTON COLLINS, owner of Dunorlan, and his family, pictured outside the house in about 1905. Collins acquired the property and its surrounding estate in 1874 when its builder, Henry Reed, returned to Australia. It later passed to his son Carteret Fitzgerald Collins, on whose death during the Second World War his family sold it to the Council.

RICHARD LATTER displaying his plaited beard which, at over sixteen feet in length, was the longest in Europe. He was born in Pembury in 1831 and died at Royal Tunbridge Wells in 1914. At the time of this picture, published as a postcard in 1908 by tobacconist R. Scales of Victoria Road, he was living in George Street. Latter has a place in the Guinness Book of Records, although some doubt is cast on the accuracy of the beard's measurement.

THE MONUMENT ERECTED IN ST JOHN'S ROAD in 1897 in memory of Canon Edward Hoare (1812–94), vicar of Holy Trinity from 1853 until his death. Once described as the 'Protestant pontiff of Tunbridge Wells', he was an outstanding preacher and took a leading part in local affairs. 'At his funeral all public bodies Civil and Religious were represented and in company with Bishops and over 100 Clergy in their robes together with prominent residents marched in procession to the Burial Place.' In 1980 a road widening scheme led to the monument being moved to a new site several yards away.

A CLASSROOM SCENE IN KING CHARLES' SCHOOL about 1906, showing in the background from right to left the headmster William A. Diggens and teachers Thomas E. Mann and Harry Braddon (who was headmaster 1921–47). The school, the first to be established in the town, was set up in 1698 by public subscription, being originally 'maintained by the charitable contributions of the nobility and gentry resorting to that place in the summer season.'

PUPILS OF KING CHARLES' SCHOOL photographed with W.A. Diggens in August 1902. Diggens served as headmaster from 1879 until his retirement in 1914. He took over the post from his father, Alfred Diggens, who served from 1856. In its early days the school met within the premises of the church and did not acquire a building of its own until 1848 after William Law Pope, the church's minister, had obtained an adjoining site. After this building became inadequate, alterations and extensions were undertaken in 1887. The school survived until 1960.

'DURING THE SEASON, an efficient band of musicians "discourse eloquent music" to the company. They perform on the Parade every morning, commencing at eleven o'clock, and at other parts of the town in the afternoon and evening.' So writes the author of Pelton's guide in 1875, about the time of this photograph. By this period the Musick Gallery seen behind, successor to that mentioned in the Rusthall Manor Act of 1739, had fallen into disuse.

THE FEDERATION BAND OF THE ROYAL TUNBRIDGE WELLS and District Band Federation, photographed in 1930. According to the town guide for that year, 'one feature of the social life at Tunbridge Wells which always forcefully appeals to visitors is the excellent series of Concerts given by Orchestral and Military Bands on the Pantiles and in the Calverley Grounds during the summer months . . . the musical programmes are not only of intrinsic merit but are rendered by accomplished instrumentalists in a manner that adds very considerably to the joys of summer-time.'

ROYAL TUNBRIDGE WELLS DRUM AND FIFE BAND, pictured on a postcard published by André Page of London Road, Southborough, about 1936. At this period the various bands of the district held an annual contest in the Calverley Grounds, described in the borough guide as 'a memorable occasion, the rival bands making a brave display during their march through the town'.

A PHOTOGRAPH ENTITLED 'High Brooms Sunday School outing' taken about 1908 by Sydney A. Baker, watchmaker and photographer, of 118 London Road, Southborough. High Brooms became an independent parish in 1902, when the present church of St Matthew was constructed. The area was previously served by a Mission Church attached to the parish of St Peter's, Southborough.

ALFRED PAGET HEDGES, the newly elected Liberal MP for the Tonbridge Division of Kent (in which Tunbridge Wells was then included), appears at a window to acknowledge the crowd gathered outside the old Town Hall following the declaration of poll in 1906. The defeated Conservative candidate, Arthur Boscawen, had served since 1892. Herbert Spender Clay regained the seat for the Conservatives at the next election in 1910, and served until 1937. The photographer was Percy Lankester.

THE TUNBRIDGE WELLS ANGLING SOCIETY'S float prepared for the Hospital Sunday parade on 21 July 1907. The procession was an annual fund-raising event organized by the local friendly societies and ended with a church service, that year at Mount Pleasant Congregational. According to a report in the local press, 'the weather was excellent from the collector's point of view, but a long and dusty march by the processionists through the town was a trying experience. But undertaken in the spirit of charity, it was cheerfully done.'

LEO, CANINE COLLECTOR FOR THE GENERAL HOSPITAL, photographed in 1906 with Molly Egginton, whose mother was a great supporter of the hospital which at this period obtained most of its income from annual subscriptions, donations, and fund-raising efforts. Her father, Colonel Egginton, who adopted the name of Mr Welton Dale, was the original joint lessee and manager of the Opera House. Leo belonged to Miss Baxter, matron of the Mount Ephraim Nursing Home in Molyneux Park.

A POSTCARD CELEBRATING THE SUCCESS of R. Arnold's 1907 collection of farthings to provide breakfasts for children of the slums in London, including an appeal for future contributions. At the time Arnold was living at 15 Mount Pleasant, part of the Great Hall complex, which was also the address of the photographer and publisher of the picture, Percy Lankester.

GROUP OF INMATES AT THE CRIPPLES' HOME, TUNBRIDGE WELLS.

SOME OF THE RESIDENTS in about 1907 of the Home for Little Incurables, Agra House, Park Road, run by the Tunbridge Wells branch of the National Incorporated Waifs' Association (Dr Barnardo's Homes). The house was purchased with funds raised locally and opened on 18 December 1902. Prominent features in local guides of the period invited subscriptions and donations and informed local residents that the 'Home is open daily to visitors, Sundays excepted, from 2.30 to 5 o'clock pm. Gifts of Clothing, Fruit, Vegetables, etc., will be thankfully received by the Matron.'

AN EMPIRE DAY CELEBRATION at the Royal Victoria School for Boys in 1907. The foundation stone of the original school building, designed by Decimus Burton, was laid on 29 September 1834 by the Princess Victoria and her mother the Duchess of Kent, who took a great interest in the work. They contributed £100 to the building fund and took part in a sale of work held on the Pantiles to raise money for the project, 'not only buying freely but also making and contributing articles for it'.

A PHOTOGRAPH BY LANKESTER of the ruins of the pavilion on the Nevill Cricket Ground after it had been burned down by suffragettes on 11 April 1913, at a time when the town was said to be 'a hotbed of militants'. Angry residents held a protest meeting at the Great Hall in May at which Sir Arthur Conan Doyle was the leading speaker. Suffragettes who arrived with placards to disrupt the meeting met with considerable hostility and had eggs thrown at them. Funds were raised quickly for a replacement pavilion which was completed just in time for Cricket Week.

MEMBERS OF C SQUADRON, the Tunbridge Wells company of the West Kent (Queen's Own) Imperial Yeomanry, in their drill hall at the Corn Exchange on the Lower Walk of the Pantiles at the time of their mobilization in August 1914. At the outbreak of war there were two

groups of Territorials based in the town, the other consisting of the D and E Companies of the 4th Battalion The Queen's Own Royal West Kent Regiment, who had their headquarters at the Drill Hall in Victoria Road.

AN EDWARDIAN VIEW OF VISITORS taking the waters at the Pantiles, published by H.G. Groves, postmaster, stationer and art dealer, whose premises on the Upper Walk were close to the Spring. By this period the medicinal value of the waters was beginning to be taken less seriously than in earlier times. According to the 1910 official guide, 'how far beneficial results to be derived from taking the waters are due to the waters, and how far they are due to the Common, and its beautiful balmy air, it would be difficult to say.'

FOLLOWING MOBILIZATION THE LOCAL TERRITORIALS left the town on Wednesday 5 August 1914. Here the West Kent Yeomanry, led by Major R.B. Pott, make their way past the Pump Room (right) towards the Central Station to join the other squadrons at Maidstone. The crowds that gathered to see them off had increased further by the time the men of the West Kent Regiment left for Dover at nine o'clock when 'the station yard, Vale-road and half-way up Mount Pleasant were thronged with a packed and excited crowd cheering and singing patriotic songs for all they were worth'.

al Tunbridge Wells

ONE OF A SERIES OF PHOTOGRAPHS BY HAROLD CAMBURN recording the Territorial Army encampment established on the Lower Cricket Ground from 10 September until the end of October 1914. Royal Tunbridge Wells had been chosen as the headquarters for a large body of Territorials whose main camp was situated at Crowborough. The detachment on the Common consisted of two signal companies. Contemporary press reports tell how the local residents came out to watch them, some bringing baskets of apples to feed the horses.

D COMPANY, THE 1ST BATTALION, the Mid Kent Volunteer Fencibles on parade on South-borough Common. Formed in March 1915 as the Southborough Company of the Tunbridge Wells Volunteer Training Corps, it consisted of men from Southborough and the neighbouring villages who were over military age or otherwise unfitted for regular service. The Fencibles were to be available in the event of invasion or if required to release other forces from home service. They were incorporated into the Royal West Kent Regiment in 1918 and disbanded in the following year.

PUPILS AT ST MARK'S CHURCH OF ENGLAND SCHOOL photographed by D.J. Johnson. The school, then in Frant Road, was opened on 15 January 1872 by the vicar of St Mark's Church, Revd F.R. Johnstone, on land provided by the Earl of Abergavenny. It was built by public subscription for 'the education of children of the labouring, manufacturing and other poor classes of the neighbourhood'. In 1987 the school moved to premises formerly occupied by Ramslye Primary School in Ramslye Road.

DR GEORGE ABBOTT (1844–1925), founder and first Curator of Tunbridge Wells Museum. In 1885 a changing display of local flora arranged by Abbott in the Literary Society's rooms at the Pantiles aroused enthusiasm for the formation of the Tunbridge Wells Natural History and Philosophical Society. An immediate aim of the Society was the formation of exhibit collections for a museum. Other local projects pioneered by Abbott included the Ear and Eye Hospital and the Technical Institute (now Adult Education Centre).

THE MUNICIPAL EDUCATIONAL MUSEUM, at 18 Crescent Road, opened in July 1918 after a long campaign by Dr Abbott to persuade the Council to adopt the Natural History Society's ever growing collections. He remained curator until his death in 1925. Prominent in the window in this view are flint implements collected by Abbott's friend Benjamin Harrison, grocer and archaeologist at Ightham. The Museum remained at this site until the lease expired in 1928. The collections were then moved to Abbotsford in Upper Grosvenor Road.

Hailstones from the Great Storm. Tunbridge Wells. 25th May 1922.
E.A. Sweetman & Son

ON THURSDAY 25 MAY 1922 THE TOWN was struck by a violent hail-storm which stripped the leaves from trees, shattered greenhouses and caused flooding in the town centre. One resident 'likened the hailstones to balls of silver as they fell through space, and the effect of the sun produced colours of a wonderful hue'. Afterwards, 'hailstones were piled up on every path and had not melted at a late hour'. Local photographers E.A. Sweetman and Son produced this card to demonstrate how large the pellets were.

HAROLD CAMBURN was also present to record the effects of the great storm. Here he captures the scene at the foot of Mount Pleasant where 'the flood steadily rose over the pavement and invaded the ground floors of all the business premises ... and flooded the basements and cellarage. Pedestrians who had helter-skelter sought the nearest refuge from the hail, found their retreat cut off ... Drivers struggled with terrifed horses which were stung by hailstones as big as pigeon eggs', and motor vehicles became stranded.

MEMBERS OF THE KING CHARLES' SCHOOL STAFF in costume as a German band. Thomas Mann is second from the right. The photograph was taken in the school yard about 1910.

THE 'CHARIOT RACE', one of the less conventional events in the King Charles' School Athletic Sports on the afternoon of Thursday 25 July 1929. The Sports were held annually at the Nevill Athletic Ground, the four houses of Rupert, Falkland, Ormonde and Montrose competing for the Clark Trophy. Besides standard athletics, the programme included a three-legged race, a leap frog race and 'mounted potato sticking'. The photograph is one of a series by Christopher Durrant of St James' Park.

THOMAS MANN (right) receives a silver teapot and cheque from Cirrol Clark on behalf of the staff and boys of King Charles' School on his retirement in December 1951. He joined the staff in November 1905 at the same time as Harry Braddon, whom he succeeded as headmaster in 1947. They, together with Clark, who arrived at the school in 1921, made up the trio of popular and long-serving masters known as the 'Three Musketeers'. Mr Clark, called 'Clackers' by the pupils, retired in 1952.

THE OFFICIAL OPENING OF TUNBRIDGE WELLS MUSEUM'S new premises at 12 Mount Ephraim by Alderman Ebenezer Saunders (fourth from right), the chairman of the Council's Library and Museum Committee, on Saturday 4 August 1934. Third from the right is the curator, Dr John C.M. Given, an amateur geologist and retired medical paractitioner who held office from 1929 until 1948. Far left is the assistant curator, Miss L.M. Child, and third from the left is the widow of the Museum's founder Dr Abbott. Three years later plans were approved to include a Library and Museum building as part of the new Civic Centre development, but, due to the War, the Museum did not move until 1954.

THE TEAM OF THE TUNBRIDGE WELLS PHYSICAL CULTURE CLUB, joint winners of the Metropolitan and Southern Amateur Gymnastic Association cup for team drill in January 1938. The members are (front row) R. Webb, E. Mitchell, Mr J. Robinson (instructor), H. Brown and G. Batchelor. Behind are J. Luker, C. Fry, H. Grinyer (pianist), J. Jennings and B. Hope. The club won several prizes and often gave exhibitions at local events, but membership declined with the beginning of the Second World War.

DAVID J. JOHNSON (1862–1945), a Tunbridge Wells photogrpaher and Mount Sion resident. Johnson briefly maintained a photography business at 1 St Johns Road before setting up the firm of Johnson, Bird, and Co. at 39 High Street. The business opened in 1900 and closed in 1928. He produced several albums of local view photographs from c.1900 to c.1930, several of which are included in this selection. As a local history source the albums are invaluable since they frequently contain obscure street scenes away from the main roads and famous sites.

THE PEOPLE OF THE TOWN gave generously toward the mayor's Spitfire Fund in 1940. By October sufficient money had been gathered to pay for 'one of the latest types of fighter planes'. The mayor, Alderman Westbrook, was able to send £5,723 to Lord Beaverbrook. Pictured here is the aeroplane *Royal Tunbridge Wells*, delivered to the RAF in April 1941.

'DON'T KEEP A SKELETON IN YOUR CUPBOARD – Let Us Call For It – We Need the Bones!' and 'If you can't get Petrol, Give Us Your Car'; two signs inducing patriots to contribute to the war effort during the Second World War. Almost anything appeared to be useful, iron, brass, bones, rags, paper, string . . . At the far right of this view are four sets of carthorse bells which were 'saved' in 1940 and were donated to Tunbridge Wells Museum in 1941.

WAITRESSES FROM BINN'S CAFE stroll along the Pantiles during Pantiles Week 1949. The week, 4 to 9 April, was a promotional idea instigated by the Pantiles Association. The shops organized special window displays, shop assistants served in eighteenth-century costume, an orchestra played at the bandstand twice daily and the Royal Tunbridge Wells Art Club held a special Pantiles exhibition. A report stated that 'the atmosphere is gay and carefree. Everyone walks with a jaunty step on the Pantiles this week.'

SPECTATORS ALONG THE HIGH STREET as Royal Tunbridge Wells witnessed its first carnival procession for fourteen years on Saturday 2 June 1951. The event marked the opening of the Tunbridge Wells Chamber of Trade Shopping Week. One of the largest and most impressive parade entries – four 3.7 anti-aircraft guns drawn by tractors and accompanied by mobile radar equipment and Land Rovers – gave a demonstration and display later on the Lower Cricket Ground.

MORE CROWDS WATCHING THE 1951 carnival procession along London Road. First prize in the procession went to the Ancient Order of Foresters' float, with second and third prizes going to the Royal Observer Corps and the Tunbridge Wells Operatic Society. One of the funniest scenes was provided on the float of the Electrical Contractors Association. Here men dressed up as buxom women showed how housework was done 100 years before.

A PHOTOGRAPH OF AN AMERICAN TROTTING HORSE DEMONSTRATION during the Tunbridge Wells and South East Counties Agricultural Show at the Eridge Road showground on 20 July 1955. In that year the two-day show attracted 24,394 visitors. Here, on the right, Freddie Chapman, amateur whipper-in for the Eridge Hunt, is seen riding behind His Lordship, an American pacing horse. Mr Chapman came second in one of the heats. In the final event he came last, 'but it was good fun — especially when he was presented with a dummy pig, borrowed from one of the trade exhibits'.

A *COURIER* PHOTOGRAPH OF THE AGRICULTURAL SHOW of June 1956. Here the most spectacular scene of the Show is in progress, the grand parade of prize-winning cattle. Herefords were shown for the first time. The Tunbridge Wells and South East Counties Agricultural Show was established in 1862 and enjoyed the patronage of the Marquess of Abergavenny for many years. The Queen Mother visited in the centenary year, taking lunch at Eridge Castle before being entertained at the Show by the president, Lord Abergavenny.

HAROLD BETTERIDGE'S VIEW OF CHIPPERFIELD'S CIRCUS on the Lower Cricket Ground. A new act for the 1962 season, The Fantasy of the Bulls, brought controversy and publicity. An advertising poster for the show depicted 'a fear-crazed bull with blood gushing from a spear wound in its shoulder'. Complaints of gross cruelty were sent to the Council and to the Manor. However, a circus spokesman pointed out that in fact blood was never spilled during the act. An accompanying picture in the *Courier* showed Doreen Duggan, who ran the act, cuddling one of the bulls.

A BOXING DAY MEET of the Eridge Foxhounds at Tunbridge Wells Common, from a photograph published in the 1960 and subsequent official guides to the town. In 1881 Lord George Nevill, third son of the Marquess of Abergavenny, became the first Master of the newly-formed West Kent Woodland pack. Later this became the Eridge Foxhounds, based at Abergavenny's seat, Eridge.

HUGH REYNOLDS, AS BEAU NASH, escorts Miss Tunbridge Wells, Heather Murrell, along the Pantiles at the opening of the Tunbridge Wells carnival on 6 July 1974 in this *Courier* picture. Other historical celebrities of Tunbridge Wells accompanying the Beau in the initial procession included Bell Causey, Sarah Porter, Prince Rupert, Nell Gwynne and George I. After being welcomed by Cllr G.J. Slater and Lieut.-Col. Reginald Smith, Nash 'thanked the throng for his warm reception ... and invited one and all to join in the dancing, raffling and games he was promoting.'

Shops and Industries

THE PANTILES VIEWED FROM THE BATH HOUSE in the 1870s or 1880s. It was the site of the first markets and shops at the Wells and is arguably the oldest pedestrian shopping precinct. With the commercial growth of Mount Pleasant and the High Street, the Pantiles has developed into a street filled primarily with specialty shops.

THE PREMISES OF STEPHEN CARWOOD, saddler and harness manufacturer at 8 London Road, photographed in about May 1900. An advertisement of the time states that Carwood's had a world-wide reputation for their vast stock of dog collars. Also, they traded in purses, bags, belts, trunks and portmanteaus, to standard designs or custom-made under the proprietor's personal supervision.

DURRANT'S, grocer, wine, spirits and beer merchant of 7 The Pantiles. The building is said to have been erected as a private dwelling in 1660, followed by conversion to Durrant's Grocery and Wine Shop in 1768. The establishment continues as a wine merchant.

THE SHOP OF ALBERT FOWLER, ironmonger, situated on Grosvenor Road, opposite the old General Hospital, at the turn of the century. Fowler's stockrooms were replete with marble and enamelled chimney pieces, tiled registers, slow combustion and other grates, tile hearths with marble, brass, and iron curbs, fire brasses and irons, kitchen ranges, stoves, cutlery, tea and coffee sets, cruet stands, lamps, etc., etc.

LOOKING EAST ALONG CALVERLEY ROAD, c.1905. Other than Waymark's prominent establishment, one can see Albert Rofe's Grosvenor Tavern (far left); Peark's Stores, grocers; Charles Kennard's tobacco and confectionery shop; Paine Smith and Co. Ltd, confectioners; and T.C. Cunningham, upholsterer, cabinet maker and undertaker. Further along, the pavement is crowded with people and wares, while stalls line the kerb.

THE CAMDEN ROAD END OF CALVERLEY ROAD during a Saturday afternoon street market. Adie's terrace to the left then had Victorian shop fronts, all of which have been replaced by ubiquitous aluminium, PVC and plate glass. Curiously, the processor of this old photograph retouched the negative to obliterate the name sign of the clothing shop second from the left.

THE IMPRESSIVE DELIVERY VAN of F. Hayden and Co., ironmongers and engineers, photographed 19 July 1916. Frederick Hayden maintained premises at 38 High Street for twenty years, being preceded there by the Usher Brothers, ironmongers, until 1913, and succeeded in 1936 by Louis G. Ford, ironmonger and builders merchant.

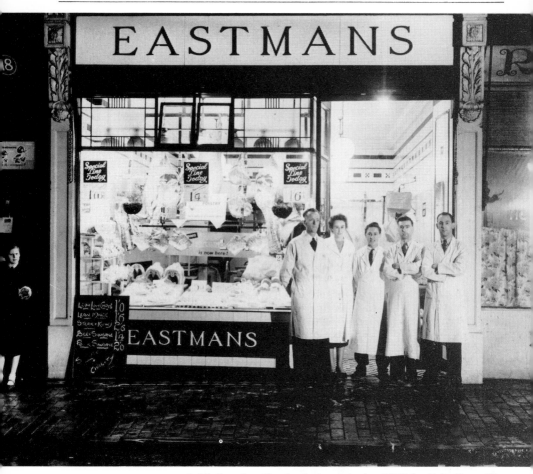

EASTMAN LTD, BUTCHERS, of 16 Camden Road, photographed c.1953 by R.J. Glass. The manager was Mr Tony Byrne (far left), assisted by Iris Byrne, Pat Baker, Ernie Osbourne and Ted Kerry. The window display shows that forty years ago one could purchase lean minced steak for 1s. 6d. per pound, choice lean chops for 1s. per pound, and steak and kidney at 2s. 6d. per pound. Service and Civility.

JOHN FRANCIS ALLEN'S LEATHER MARKET at 31 Calverley Road traded during the early years of this century. A massive display of leather footware is shown, from 2s. 11d. to 18s. 6d. per pair. The modified remains of the building were swept away along with relocation of the adjacent Burton's building facade to allow construction of an entrance for the Royal Victoria Place Shopping centre.

THE FURNISHING AND IRONMONGERY BUSINESS of Mr S. Edwin Haward at 14–18 Goods Station Road, from a Tunbridge Wells pictorial history book of 1892. Established in 1865, Haward's prosperity led to several extensions of the accommodation. A branch at 21 Mount Pleasant, new in 1892, catered for cutlery, high-class ironmongery and silverware requirements. All other ironmongery and furniture could be supplied from the main branch. Behind the Goods Station Road premises were Haward's workshops known as the Suffolk Works.

LOOKING NORTH ALONG the upper part of the High Street in about 1905 from a postcard produced by Harold Camburn. The terrace to the right was built in the grounds of South Grove House by William Willicombe in the 1850s. At 37 High Street, originally numbered 3 South Grove Terrace, the clock of Payne and Son was a landmark, as it has been since this branch of the business was opened by Thomas Edward Payne in 1871.

LOOKING NORTH ALONG THE HIGH STREET, 26 May 1990. Close examination shows that little of consequence has changed in the streetscape here in ninety years. Bicycles, a waggon, carts and one car were once the only conveyances. Now cars line the street, and anyone strolling down the centre of the road is likely to be injured.

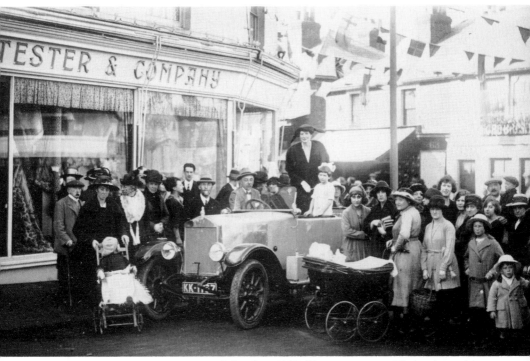

THE OPENING DAY OF SHOPPING WEEK, 16 October 1922. The streets were filled with window shoppers searching for lucky numbers secreted in shop windows entitling them to free gifts. Behind this crowd in Camden Road are the extensive premises of John Tester and Company, drapers, and Dartford Brewery's public house The Foresters.

THE PREMISES AT 9 CHAPEL PLACE of Mr F. Larkin, family butcher. In 1892 Larkin's business was thriving, with shops also at Calverley Road and Mount Sion. Larkin was said to be well known as a purveyor of first-class meats, notably Southdown mutton and lamb. 'Well-fed meats of every description' were available, along with 'personal attention to all details of business, and prompt attention to orders from town or country'.

THE TOP OF MOUNT PLEASANT ROAD, c.1905, showing in the background the Opera House and Calverley Parade. The double-decker omnibus of the Tunbridge Wells, Southborough and District Omnibus Co. Ltd has just driven up from the Central Station, and the leading third horse is being released.

THE SPACIOUS CARRIAGE OF DURTNALLS LTD removers at Vale Royal, photographed by D.J. Johnson on 18 June 1934. Established in 1812, Durtnalls Ltd (Furniture) Depositories had premises at 35 London Road as well as offices at London, Worthing and the head office at Brighton. By the time of this photograph, the company was no longer dependent upon horses and waggons. They also employed a fleet of lorries and vans.

THE APPROPRIATELY DECORATED PREMISES OF FRANK ROSIER, wood carver and cabinet maker of Frant. He was active from 1903 until the early 1940s, and was considered by some as the natural inheritor of the mantle of Grinling Gibbons. Rosier's work can be found in Frant Church, Mayfield Church and a number of houses in the area. In 1923 the *Tunbridge Wells Magazine* stated that two years before the First World War Rosier 'was reluctantly persuaded to send an example of his art to Olympia, and the result was that he won a bronze medal against the world'.

CRICKET BALLS HAVE BEEN MADE LOCALLY since 1760 when Duke and Son shoe makers of Penshurst set up a separate business for their manufacture. Later, workshops of other manufacturers were set up at Southborough and Tonbridge. At his Southborough premises T.K. Twort significantly advanced ball design when he perfected a ball having the thickness of leather at the seams no greater than that elsewhere. Here a seamer is putting on the first or centre seam of a cricket ball.

THE PREMISES OF THE *TUNBRIDGE WELLS ADVERTISER* newspaper, and the shop of Mr R.H.M. Clements, printer and stationer, at the bottom of Grove Hill Road, opened in 1897 and here photographed in 1935. Robert Clements became editor of the *Advertiser* in 1881, taking over as proprietor shortly afterwards. Through his newspaper, Clements influenced many town developments including incorporation, the acquisition of Calverley Grounds, slum clearances, 'cottages for the working classes', and smoking concerts in the Great Hall to entertain Great War soldiers stationed in the town.

THE RECEPTION OF THE LONDON AND COUNTIES DISTRIBUTING COMPANY'S first goods car to enter Tunbridge Wells on 7 June 1901, photographed by Percy Lankester. From a base in London at the Spur Inn Yard, the Company intended to 'send a line of steam waggons, travelling at an average speed of five miles an hour, to Tunbridge Wells and intermediate towns, for the conveyance of goods of various descriptions. Their great object is quickness of delivery.' The local receiving office would be at Southborough, from which vans would disperse to deliver the bales, boxes and barrels. The journey of this first waggon was both an

exhibition and trial run for the service, unfortunately marred by delays due to a broken pump. Gentlemen traders assembled, along with much of the population of Southborough, to receive the waggon at the corner of Speldhurst Road. Mr H.J. Willmot, president of the Tradesmen's Association, welcomed the waggon and the Company's directors to the town before the vehicle proceeded as far as the Pantiles. In the evening one of the directors, Mr Walter Phillips, marked the inauguration of the service by a dinner at the Swan Hotel for all who supported this new enterprise.

JOHN BROWN (1845–1934), founder in 1870 of the John Brown Dairies. In 1898 Brown sold the dairy business and became a co-director with Messrs Buss and Peters of the Opera House Company. From 1905 to 1918 Brown represented the South Ward on the Town Council, standing unopposed in 1906, 1909 and 1912. For thirty years John Brown was manager and director of the Nevill Bakery, with premises in Nevill Street and High Street. Although a genial man, Brown had a reputation as a hard taskmaster who expected his employees to work as hard and as long as himself.

A JOHN BROWN'S DAIRIES DELIVERY CART. As Brown's dairy business prospered, the business merged with other dairies and took over farms, eventually controlling shops at Vale Road, the Pantiles and St Johns Road, and farms at Ramslye, Great Culverden, Mount Ephraim and Frant. An account of 1892 states that a large staff of assistants was employed 'under first-class personal and sanitary direction' and 'under strictly medical supervision' in processing and distributing the milk which was 'sent to all parts of the town twice daily'.

GEORGE WILLIAM BURROWS, the last of that name in the business of Tunbridge ware manufacture, photographed by H. Jenkins in 1898. James Burrows acquired the business of Mr Jordan in about 1740. The mosaic technique now generally synonymous with Tunbridge ware was not developed until the time of Burrows's grandsons. William worked at Gibraltar Cottage, Humphrey at Jordan House and George and James had their manufactory at Hanover Road. The mosaic process seems to have been developed by the latter James Burrows late in the 1820s.

HENRY HOLLAMBY was apprenticed to George and James Burows in 1831 and set up his own business in about 1842. Hollamby practised mainly the standard mosaic technique of the ware, producing many large blocks depicting local topographical views. In the 1880s he employed as many as forty hands at his Frant Road manufactory.

THE CHALET, MOUNT EPHRAIM, the Tunbridge ware manufactory of Thomas Barton. The premises had been occupied from the late eighteenth century by William Fenner, and from 1840 by Edmund Nye. Having worked for many years with Edmund Nye as his partner and designer, Barton took over the firm shortly before Nye's death in 1863. As well as producing distinctive mosaic ware, Barton also produced transfer-printed wares, marquetry and parquetry.

R.J. SHARVILL, bandmaker for the firm of Boyce, Brown and Kemp. Thomas Amos Boyce, James Brown and John Kemp formed a partnership in 1873 and set up premises in Camden Road. The firm produced mosaic Tunbridge ware views of many local sites similar to those of Hollamby, including Eridge Castle, the Pantiles, Penshurst Place, Hever Castle and Battle Abbey. When Hollamby's manufactory closed in 1891, Boyce, Brown and Kemp purchased the remaining stock. At the death of Thomas Barton in 1903 the firm remained as the only Tunbridge ware manufacturers. It survived until 1927.

THE CULVERDEN BREWERY OF E. AND H. KELSEY LTD viewed from St John's Church in 1949. Edward and Henry Kelsey formed the business in 1855. By the time of Henry's retirement in 1895, the firm owned over 100 public houses in Kent, Sussex and Surrey. A year before this picture was taken, Kelsey's was taken over by J.W. Green and Co., which subsequently became Flowers Breweries Ltd. A.R. Kelsey continued to be chairman until his death in 1962 when the Culverden Brewery was closed.

JOHN PEARSON'S SHOEING FORGE at Kelseys Cottages, off St John's Road. Pearson also had a forge at Hope Terrace. The business flourished until about 1920. The cottages, to the left in this photograph, and the forge itself, have been replaced by a car park.

FARRIERS AT ANOTHER FORGE, possibly the one which stood at Fonthill, opposite the Pantiles on London Road, until the Fonthill rest shelter was built in 1939. Next door was the former Elliott's Carriage Works, succeeded by the business of W.T. Noakes, where fine landaus, phaetons and dog-carts were available for inspection and purchase.

HOP PICKERS photographed by S.K. Lazell. Nowadays nearly all hops are harvested by machinery, but machines did not come into general use until the 1950s. Hop pickers came for the season from London and farther afield, often being accommodated in very primitive conditions. Gypsies came also, bringing their own quarters.

A PHOTOGRAPH dated 1934, from the Johnson album, of J. Rawson and Sons Ltd, motor engineers, at 11 London Road facing Mount Sion Road. At this time Rawsons provided 'the complete service to motorists', and their range of cars included models of Armstrong-Siddeley, Austin, Humber, Morris and Riley. The business opened at these premises in 1913.

A VIEW dated 1974, from the *Courier* along the western end of Calverley Road, the section which was converted into a pedestrian precinct in 1986. On the right is the terrace by Adie. The assortment of buildings on the left includes the distinctive Burton facade of about 1929. The British Home Stores stands on the site of the original Baptist Tabernacle of 1883, demolished about 1938 when the congregation moved to new premises in Upper Grosvenor Road.

ACKNOWLEDGEMENTS

We are grateful to the following people for assistance during the research for this book: Mr R. Farthing, Mrs J. Holloway and Miss J. Mauldon. For permission to reproduce photographs we thank: Mr R.J. Glass, the *Kent and Sussex Courier* newspaper and Mr B. Lazell. Every effort has been made to obtain permission to reproduce those photographs covered by copyright.